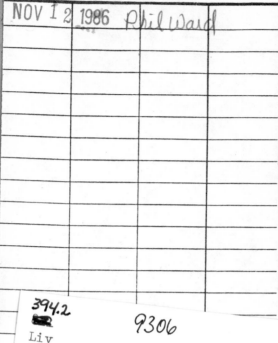

D1011347

Callooh! Callay!

HOLIDAY POEMS
FOR YOUNG READERS

Callooh! Callay!

HOLIDAY POEMS
FOR YOUNG READERS

edited by
MYRA COHN LIVINGSTON

illustrated by Janet Stevens

A Margaret K. McElderry Book

Atheneum   1980   New York

For Mary Handelsman and *our* children at Beverly Vista

Library of Congress catalog card number: 78-8794
ISBN 0-689-50117-X
Copyright © 1978 by Myra Cohn Livingston
All rights reserved
Published simultaneously in Canada
by McClelland & Stewart, Ltd.
Printed and bound by
American Book—Stratford Press
Saddle Brook, New Jersey
Designed by Marjorie Zaum
First Printing September 1978
Second Printing March 1980

ACKNOWLEDGEMENTS

The editor and publisher thank the following for permission to reprint the copyrighted material listed below:

ATHENEUM PUBLISHERS FOR "Conversation Hearts" from ALL THE DAY LONG by Nina Payne, text copyright © 1973 by Nina Payne; "We Three" from SEE MY LOVELY POISON IVY by Lilian Moore, text copyright © 1975 by Lilian Moore; "Happy Birthday to Me" from CATCH A LITTLE RHYME by Eve Merriam, copyright © 1966 by Eve Merriam; "Which Washington," "To Meet Mr. Lincoln" and "A Secret" from THERE IS NO RHYME FOR SILVER by Eve Merriam, copyright © 1962 by Eve Merriam; "A Monstrous Mouse" from ONE WINTER NIGHT IN AUGUST And Other Nonsense Jingles by X. J. Kennedy (A Margaret K. McElderry Book), copyright © 1975 by X. J. Kennedy; "12 October" and "Father" from THE MALIBU And Other Poems by Myra Cohn Livingston (A Margaret K. McElderry Book), copyright © 1972 by Myra Cohn Livingston; "First Thanksgiving" from 4-WAY STOP And Other Poems by Myra Cohn Livingston; (A Margaret K. McElderry Book), copyright © 1976 by Myra Cohn Livingston; "When I am a man" from SONGS OF THE DREAM PEOPLE: Chants and Images from the Indians and Eskimos of North America edited by James Houston (A Margaret K. McElderry Book), copyright © 1972 by James Houston.

BRANDT & BRANDT for "Abraham Lincoln" from A BOOK OF AMERICANS by Rosemary and Stephen Vincent Benet; Holt, Rinehart and Winston, Inc.; copyright 1933 by Stephen Vincent Benet, copyright renewed, 1961, by Rosemary Carr Benet.

WILLIAM COLLINS & WORLD PUBLISHING CO., INC. for "You'll find whenever the New Year comes" from CHINESE MOTHER GOOSE RHYMES by Robert Wyndham, copyright © 1968 by Robert Wyndham.

SIMON CAMPBELL for "I will go with my Father a-ploughing" and "Harvest Song" by Joseph Campbell.

HILDA CONKLING for "Easter" from "Poems By A Little Girl" by Hilda Conkling: Stokes—J. B. Lippincott—1920—All rights 1947—Hilda Conkling.

THOMAS Y. CROWELL COMPANY for "Huckleberry, gooseberry, raspberry pie," "Happy Birthday Silly Goose," "Country Bumpkin," and

ACKNOWLEDGEMENTS

"Apples for the Little One" from FATHER FOX'S PENNYRHYMES by Clyde Watson, illustrated by Wendy Watson. Copyright © 1971 by Clyde Watson.

CURTIS BROWN, LTD. for "Written on an Egg" by Eduard Mörike, translated by Doris Orgel, from CRICKET, Vol. 2, No. 9, copyright © 1975 by Open Court Publishing Co.; "Little Catkins" by Alexander Blok, translated by Babette Deutsch, copyright © 1966 from TWO CENTURIES OF RUSSIAN VERSE, edited by Avram Yarmolinsky, published by Random House, Inc. 1966.

DOUBLEDAY & COMPANY, INC. for "Fourth of July" from A LITTLE BOOK OF DAYS by Rachel Field, copyright 1927 by Rachel Field.

FARRAR, STRAUS & GIROUX, INC. for "Fireworks" and "Pumpkin" from MORE SMALL POEMS by Valerie Worth, copyright © 1976 by Valerie Worth; "Sam's World" by Sam Cornish, from NATURAL PROCESS edited by Ted Wilentz and Tom Weatherly, copyright © 1970 by Hill and Wang (now Farrar, Straus & Giroux, Inc.).

HARCOURT BRACE JOVANOVICH, INC. for "Easter Eggs" and "Christmas Morning" from WINDY MORNING by Harry Behn, copyright, 1953, by Harry Behn; "Hallowe'en" from THE LITTLE HILL by Harry Behn, copyright, 1949, by Harry Behn, renewed 1977, by Alice L. Behn; "Mysterious Biography" from GOOD MORNING, AMERICA by Carl Sandburg, copyright, 1928, 1956, by Carl Sandburg; Excerpt from "Good Night" in SMOKE AND STEEL by Carl Sandburg, copyright © 1920 by Harcourt Brace Jovanovich, Inc., copyright © 1948 by Carl Sandburg; Excerpt from "Washington Monument by Night" from SLABS OF THE SUNBURNT WEST by Carl Sandburg, copyright © 1922 by Harcourt Brace Jovanovich, Inc., copyright © 1950 by Carl Sandburg: Excerpt from THE PEOPLE, YES by Carl Sandburg, copyright © 1936, by Harcourt Brace Jovanovich, Inc., copyright © 1964 by Carl Sandburg; "your birthday comes to tell me this" "hist whist" and "little tree" from COMPLETE POEMS 1913-62 by E. E. Cummings, copyright 1951 by E. E. Cummings.

HARPER & ROW, PUBLISHERS, INC. for "Otto" from BRONZEVILLE BOYS AND GIRLS by Gwendolyn Brooks, copyright © 1956 by Gwendolyn Brooks Blakely; Excerpt from "No. 4, Religion Back Home" from

Acknowledgements

ALLEGIANCES by William Stafford, copyright © 1966 by William Stafford; "The Fourth" and "Oh Have You Heard" from WHERE THE SIDEWALK ENDS by Shel Silverstein, copyright © 1974 by Shel Silverstein.

HOLT, RINEHART AND WINSTON for "July" from EVERETT ANDERSON'S YEAR by Lucille Clifton, copyright © 1974 by Lucille Clifton; "My Name" from KIM'S PLACE by Lee Bennett Hopkins. Copyright © 1974 by Lee Bennett Hopkins; "For Allan" from ROBERT FROST POETRY AND PROSE edited by Edward Connery Lathem and Lawrance Thompson. Copyright © 1972 by Holt, Rinehart and Winston.

LONGMAN CANADA LIMITED for "When I am a man," translated by Franz Boaz, from SONGS OF THE DREAM PEOPLE: *Chants and Images from the Indians and Eskimos of North America* edited by James Houston.

ALFRED A. KNOPF, INC. for "February" from A CHILD'S CALENDAR, by John Updike, illustrated by Nancy Burkert. Copyright © 1965 by John Updike and Nancy Burkert. "Refugee in America" copyright 1943 by The Curtis Publishing Company. Reprinted from SELECTED POEMS, by Langston Hughes. "Mother to Son" copyright 1926 by Alfred A. Knopf, Inc. and renewed 1954 by Langston Hughes. Reprinted from SELECTED POEMS, by Langston Hughes. "Lincoln Monument: Washington" from THE DREAM KEEPER *And Other Poems,* by Langston Hughes, copyright 1932 by Alfred A. Knopf, Inc. and renewed 1960 by Langston Hughes.

KARLA KUSKIN for "The Porcupine" by Karla Kuskin.

J. B. LIPPINCOTT COMPANY for "News! News!" Copyright 1938 by Eleanor Farjeon. Copyright © renewed 1966 by Gervase Farjeon. From POEMS FOR CHILDREN. Copyright 1951 by Eleanor Farjeon. "A Wish" copyright 1926, renewed 1954 by Eleanor Farjeon. From POEMS FOR CHILDREN. Copyright 1951 by Eleanor Farjeon.

LITTLE, BROWN AND COMPANY for "Easter Morning" from AWAY AND AGO by David McCord, copyright © 1968 by David McCord; "Christmas Eve" from THE STAR IN THE PAIL by David McCord, copyright © 1975 by David McCord; "Yankee Doodle" from AMERICAN FOLK POETRY.

DAVID McCORD for "Perambulator Poem" by David McCord.

ACKNOWLEDGEMENTS

NEW DIRECTIONS for "The Last Day of the Year" by Su Tung P'o from ONE HUNDRED POEMS FROM THE CHINESE by Kenneth Rexroth, copyright © 1971 by Kenneth Rexroth, all rights reserved; "The Great Mother" from TURTLE ISLAND by Gary Snyder, copyright © 1972 by Gary Snyder.

HAROLD OBER ASSOCIATES for "News! News!," copyright © 1938 by Eleanor Farjeon from POEMS FOR CHILDREN by Eleanor Farjeon, copyright © 1951 by Eleanor Farjeon; "A Wish" from POEMS FOR CHILDREN by Eleanor Farjeon, copyright © 1951 by Eleanor Farjeon; "Carol of the Brown King" by Langston Hughes from THE CRISIS, copyright © 1958 by Crisis Publishing Company.

G. P. PUTNAM'S SONS for "Fourth of July Night" from HOP, SKIP AND JUMP by Dorothy Aldis. Copyright 1934 by Dorothy Aldis; renewed.

RANDOM HOUSE, INC. for "Valentines" from PLAY EBONY, PLAY IVORY, by Henry Dumas, edited by Eugene B. Redmond. Copyright © 1974 by Loretta Dumas.

CHARLES SCRIBNER'S SONS for "The Fifth of July" from I HEAR YOU SMILING AND OTHER POEMS and "Hallow'en Witches" from AT THE TOP OF MY VOICE by Felice Holman, copyright © 1970, 1973 by Felice Holman.

IAN SERAILLIER for excerpt from "Suppose You Met a Witch" from BELINDA AND THE SWANS by Ian Seraillier, Jonathan Cape Edition, copyright © 1952 by Ian Seraillier.

SMITHSONIAN INSTITUTION PRESS for "An Indian Hymn of Thanks to Mother Corn" from Bureau of American Ethnology 22nd Annual Report, Part II: "The Hako: A Pawnee Ceremony": Alice C. Fletcher: Smithsonian Institution Press: Washington, D.C.: 1904.

UNIVERSITY OF MASSACHUSETTS PRESS for "That Dark Other Mountain" by Robert Francis from COUNT OUT INTO THE SUN (University of Massachusetts Press, 1972), copyright © 1943, 1971 by Robert Francis.

VIKING PRESS for "Father's Story," "The Circus," and "Christmas Morning" from UNDER THE TREE by Elizabeth Madox Roberts. Copyright 1922 by B. W. Huebsch, Inc., 1950 by Ivor S. Roberts.

Contents

CONTENTS

Callooh! Callay!

HOLIDAY POEMS
FOR YOUNG READERS

New Year's Day

The roads are very dirty, my boots are very thin,
I have a little pocket to put a penny in.
    God send you happy, God send you happy,
    Pray God send you a happy New-Year!

Old English Carol

A WISH

A glad New Year to all!—
Since many a tear,
Do what we can, must fall,
The greater need to wish a glad
                    New Year.

Since lovely youth is brief,
O girl and boy,
And no one can escape a share of grief,
I wish you joy;

Since hate is with us still,
I wish men love;
I wish, since hovering hawks still strike to kill,
The coming of the dove;

And since the ghouls of terror and despair
Are still abroad,
I wish the world once more within the care
Of those who have seen God.

Eleanor Farjeon

You'll find whenever the New Year comes
The Kitchen God will want some plums.
The girls will want some flowers new;
The boys will want firecrackers, too.
A new felt cap will please papa,
And a sugar cake for dear mama.

Chinese Mother Goose Rhyme

NEW YEAR'S WATER

Here we bring new water from the well so clear,
For to worship God with, this happy New Year.
Sing levy dew, sing levy dew, the water and the wine,
With seven bright gold wires, and bugles that do shine.
Since reign of fair maid, with gold upon her toe,
Open you the west door, and turn the Old Year go.
Sing reign of fair maid, with gold upon her chin,
Open you the east door, and let the New Year in.

Traditional, Welsh

NEWS! NEWS!

News! news! I bring you good news!
What will you give me, good wife, for good news!
    A cake or a groat,
    A staff or a coat,
Or a pair of your castaway shoes—for my news!
I went through the lowland
Upon the New Year,
And saw the first aconite
Shining so clear.
    Let the day blow
    With sleet and with snow,
    There's life in the lowland
    Upon the New Year!

I went round the upland
Upon the New Year,
And heard the first bleating
A-calling so clear.
    Let the night fall
    Hoar-frost and all,
    There's life on the upland,
    God Bless the New Year!
News! news! I come with good news!
What will you give me, for good news?
    A bench by your fire,
    A bed in your byre,
And a bowl when your old woman brews, for my news!

Eleanor Farjeon

THE LAST DAY OF THE YEAR

The year about to end
Is like a snake creeping in a field.
You have no sooner seen it
Than it has half disappeared.
It is gone and its trouble is gone with it.
It would be worse if you could catch it by its tail.
Why bother to try when it will do you no good?
The children are awake, they can't sleep.
They sit up all night laughing and chattering.
The cocks do not cry to announce the dawn.
The watch do not beat on their drums.
Everybody stays up while the lamps burn low,
And goes out to watch the stars fade and set.
I hope next year will be better than last.
But I know it will be just the
Same old mistakes and mischances.
Maybe I will have accomplished
More next New Year's Eve.
I should. I am still young and full of confidence.

Su Tung P'o
Translated by Kenneth Rexroth

St. Valentine's Day

From: HAMLET, ACT IV, Scene v

To-morrow is Saint Valentine's day,
    All in the morning betime,
And I a maid at your window
    To be your Valentine.

William Shakespeare

From: FATHER FOX'S PENNYRHYMES

Country Bumpkin
Pick a pumpkin
Put it in your cart:
For little Jenny
Half-a-penny
Valentine sweetheart.

Clyde Watson

Huckleberry, gooseberry, raspberry pie
All sweetest things one cannot buy.
Peppermint candies are six for a penny,
But true love & kisses, one cannot buy any.

Clyde Watson

CONVERSATION HEARTS

In February, bring them home,
pink, yellow, lavender
and lime pastels
BE MINE   I'M YOURS
to be read by the tongue
that licks the chalk
and tastes what it spells.

I'll give you a boxful
tasting of daphne, lupin,
mint and columbine;
a mouthful of secrets,
lovelier than whispers,
dear ones, friends
I'M YOURS   BE MINE

Nina Payne

A SECRET

Somebody rang the bell.

You run and look and find
A Valentine
That isn't signed.

Now who could it be?

Oh,
Even though I know—
I won't tell.

(Because, you see,
It was me.)

Eve Merriam

THE PORCUPINE

A porcupine looks somewhat silly,
He also is extremely quilly
And if he shoots a quill at you
Run fast
Or you'll be quilly too.

I would not want a porcupine
To be my loving valentine.

Karla Kuskin

FEBRUARY

The sun rides higher
   Every trip.
The sidewalk shows,
   Icicles drip.

A snowstorm comes,
   And cars are stuck,
And ashes fly
   From the old town truck.

The chickadees
   Grow plump on seed
That Mother pours
   Where they can feed.

And snipping, snipping
   Scissors run
To cut out hearts
   For everyone.

John Updike

VALENTINES

Forgive me if I have not sent you
a valentine
but I thought you knew
that you already have my heart
Here take the space where my
heart goes
I give that to you too

Henry Dumas

Birthdays

Monday's child is fair of face,
Tuesday's child is full of grace,
Wednesday's child is full of woe,
Thursday's child has far to go,
Friday's child is loving and giving,
Saturday's child works hard for a living,
And the child that is born on the Sabbath Day
Is bonny and blithe, and good and gay.

Traditional

PERAMBULATOR POEM

When I was christened
they held me up
and poured some water
out of a cup.

The trouble was
it fell on me,
and I and water
don't agree.

A lot of christeners
stood and listened:
I let them know
that I was christened.

David McCord

From: FATHER FOX'S PENNYRHYMES

Happy Birthday, Silly Goose!
Just today we'll let you loose
But if tomorrow you are hooked,
Then my dear, your goose is cooked.

Clyde Watson

HAPPY BIRTHDAY TO ME

It's my birthday
And everyone says
I'm growing up.

But look—
My arms are growing down!
See my last year's sleeves?

Eve Merriam

A MONSTROUS MOUSE

Just as I'd sucked in wind to take
A giant puff at my birthday cake,

While all the children sang and cheered,
Up shot the window shade—in peered

A monstrous mouse with jagged jaws!
Into the kitchen poked two paws

With fingernails like reindeer antlers!
The way a team of house-dismantlers

Bash houses down with a swinging ball,
He kicked—boom!—no more kitchen wall—

And through a new door to our kitchen
That wicked mouse, his whiskers twitchin',

Grabbed hold of my cake plate by both handles
And shouted, "Yum! what nice hot candles!"

Straight through my cake his head went—squish!
I didn't have time to make a wish.

But when he pulled himself back out,
All fresh fruit frosting, his whole snout

Was fire! Sparks spluttered from each whisker!
You never did see mouse-dancing brisker.

Thick clouds of smoke choked our apartment.
My father phoned the Fire Department.

Up screeched four fire trucks, sirens roaring—
Nobody found *my* party boring!

Our bowl of orangeade and ice
Proved just the thing for dunking mice.

Mouse ran outside and down his tunnel
Faster than water through a funnel.

I sort of forget what games we played.
Nobody drank much orangeade.

X. J. Kennedy

your birthday comes to tell me this

—each luckiest of lucky days
i've loved,shall love,do love you,was

and will be and my birthday is

e.e. cummings

MY NAME

I wrote my name on the sidewalk
But the rain washed it away.

I wrote my name on my hand
But the soap washed it away.

I wrote my name on the birthday card
I gave to Mother today

And there it will stay
For Mother never throws

ANYTHING

of mine away!

Lee Bennett Hopkins

Lincoln's Birthday

LINCOLN MONUMENT: WASHINGTON

Let's go see Old Abe
Sitting in the marble and the moonlight,
Sitting lonely in the marble and the moonlight,
Quiet for ten thousand centuries, old Abe.
Quiet for a million, million years.

Quiet——

And yet a voice forever
Against the
Timeless walls
Of time—
Old Abe.

Langston Hughes

TO MEET MR. LINCOLN

If I lived at the time
That Mr. Lincoln did,
And I met Mr. Lincoln
With his stovepipe lid

And his coalblack cape
And his thundercloud beard,
And worn and sad-eyed
He appeared:

"Don't worry, Mr. Lincoln,"
I'd reach up and pat his hand,
"We've got a fine president
For this land;

And the Union will be saved,
And the slaves will go free;
And you will live forever
In our nation's memory."

Eve Merriam

ABRAHAM LINCOLN
1809–1865

Lincoln was a long man.
He liked out of doors.
He liked the wind blowing
And the talk in country stores.

He liked telling stories,
He liked telling jokes.
"Abe's quite a character,"
Said quite a lot of folks.

Lots of folks in Springfield
Saw him every day,
Walking down the street
In his gaunt, long way.

Shawl around his shoulders,
Letters in his hat.
"That's Abe Lincoln."
They thought no more than that.

Knew that he was honest,
Guessed that he was odd,
Knew he had a cross wife
Though she was a Todd.

Knew he had three boys
Who liked to shout and play,
Knew he had a lot of debts
It took him years to pay.

Knew his clothes and knew his house.
"That's his office, here.
Blame good lawyer, on the whole,
Though he's sort of queer.

"Sure, he went to Congress, once.
But he didn't stay.
Can't expect us all to be
Smart as Henry Clay.

"Need a man for troubled times?
Well, I guess we do.
Wonder who we'll ever find?
Yes—I wonder who."

That is how they met and talked,
Knowing and unknowing.
Lincoln was the green pine.
Lincoln kept on growing.

Rosemary and Stephen Vincent Benét

Washington's Birthday

WHICH WASHINGTON?

There are many Washingtons:
Which one do you like best?
The rich man with his powdered wig
And silk brocaded vest?

The sportsman from Virginia
Riding with his hounds,
Sounding a silver trumpet
On the green resplendent grounds?

The President with his tricorn hat
And polished leather boots,
With scarlet capes and ruffled shirts
And fine brass-buttoned suits?

Or the patchwork man with ragged feet,
Freezing at Valley Forge,
Richer in courage than all of them—
Though all of them were George.

Eve Merriam

YANKEE DOODLE

Father and I went down to camp
Along with Captain Goodwin,
And there we saw the men and boys
As thick as hasty pudding.

Yankee Doodle, keep it up,
Yankee Doodle dandy!
Mind the music and the steps,
And with the girls be handy!

There was Captain Washington
Upon a slapping stallion,
Giving orders to his men,
I guess there was a million.

And there they had a swamping gun
As big as a log of maple,
On a deuced little cart,
A load for father's cattle.

And every time they fired it off,
It took a horn of powder;
It made a noise like father's gun,
Only a nation louder.

And there I saw a little keg,
Its heads were made of leather—
They knocked upon it with little sticks
To call the folks together.

The troopers, too, would gallop up
And fire right in our faces,
It scared me almost half to death
To see them run such races.

But I can't tell you half I saw,
They kept up such a smother,
So I took off my hat, made a bow,
And scampered home to mother.

    Yankee Doodle, keep it up,
    Yankee Doodle dandy!
    Mind the music and the steps,
    And with the girls be handy!

Traditional, American

From: WASHINGTON MONUMENT BY NIGHT

5

The wind bit hard at Valley Forge one Christmas.
Soldiers tied rags on their feet.
Red footprints wrote on the snow . . .
. . . and stone shoots into stars here
. . . into half-moon mist tonight.

6

Tongues wrangled dark at a man.
He buttoned his overcoat and stood alone.
In a snowstorm, red hollyberries, thoughts,
    he stood alone.

7

Women said: He is lonely
. . . fighting . . . fighting . . . eight years . . .

8

The name of an iron man goes over the world.
It takes a long time to forget an iron man.

Carl Sandburg

LITTLE CATKINS

Little boys and little maidens
Little candles, little catkins
    Homeward bring.

Little lights are burning softly,
People cross themselves in passing—
    Scent of spring.

Little wind so bold and merry,
Little raindrops, don't extinguish
    These flames, pray!

I will rise tomorrow, early,
Rise to greet you, Willow Sunday,
    Holy day.

        Alexander Blok
        Translated from the Russian by Babette Deutsch

EASTER

On Easter morn
Up the faint cloudy sky
I hear the Easter bell,
    Ding dong . . . ding dong . . .
Easter morning scatters lilies
On every doorstep;
Easter morning says a glad thing
Over and over.
Poor people, beggars, old women
Are hearing the Easter bell . . .
    Ding dong . . . ding dong . . .

Hilda Conkling

WRITTEN ON AN EGG

Since Easter was a month ago,
Is this an Easter egg? Well, no—
Or—yes, why not?   For who dares say
That hares do not lay eggs in May?
Scramble it, or boil, or fry it,
Any way you choose to try it.
May you get a great big lift
From my belated Easter gift,
On which I've scribbled, 'round the middle,
An up-to-now unanswered riddle
That silly fools and wise old sages
Have thought and fought about for ages:
Which came first?   The egg?   The hen?
I hereby solve it with my pen:
The egg, the egg! It was created
Hundreds of years before the hen——
Yes, but who could have laid it then?

The Easter bunny laid it!

Eduard Mörike
Translated from the German by Doris Orgel

EASTER MORNING

Is Easter just a day of hats,
Or Easter eggs from Bunny?
Is church on Easter something that's
Tomorrow if it's sunny?

You know the date: first Sunday—well?
"To follow the first full moon . . ."
"That follows the Vernal Equi—tell
Me!" . . . "nox!" That's pretty soon:

That's *very* soon! Oh, Easter means
The goddess of the spring
Who supervised the gardens, greens,
Birds, flowers, everything.

But Easter, oh, it means much more:
Christ risen from the dead;
His spirit in the heart before
We lose it in the head;

The resurrection of our love,
Compassion—sharing joy
In gratitude that we are of
This world: a girl, a boy.

David McCord

WHAT IF

Oh, what if the Easter Bunny
    should shed his pink ears?
    his white fur?
    should leap away?
    never leaving an egg?
    never weaving a basket?
Oh, what if the Easter Bunny
    should turn into a
    March Hare?

Myra Cohn Livingston

EASTER EGGS

Who in the world would ever have guessed
Over our garden wall toward town
Under the grass there's a cozy nest
Woven of weeds and twigs and down,
A nest with a pair of blue eggs in it
Spotted a little with brown.

It might be the nest of a wren or a linnet,
Is what my father said to me
As he smiled at the morning sun for a minute
And looked way up in a leafy tree,
A tree where he really thought it best
For the nest of a bird to be.

And he guessed if children looked and found
An Easter bunny hopping round
With a basket of colored eggs this season
That very well might be the reason
For a nest in the grass on the ground.

Harry Behn

April Fool's Day, May Day, The Fair and The Circus

OH HAVE YOU HEARD

Oh have you heard it's time for vaccinations?
I think someone put salt into your tea.
They're giving us eleven-month vacations.
And Florida has sunk into the sea.

Oh have you heard the President has measles?
The principal has just burned down the school.
Your hair is full of ants and purple weasels—
      APRIL FOOL!

Shel Silverstein

The fair maid who, on the first day of May
Goes to the fields at break of day,
And washes in dew from the hawthorn tree,
Will ever after handsome be.

Old Proverb

From: THE RURAL DANCE ABOUT THE
        MAYPOLE

Come lasses and lads,
Take leave of your dads,
And away to the Maypole hey;
      For every he
      Has got him a she
      With a minstrel standing by;
For Willy has gotten his Jill,
And Jenny has got his Jone,
To jig it, jig it, jig it, jig it,
Jig it up and down.

Traditional, English

From: THE MAY QUEEN

You must wake and call me early, call me early,
    mother dear;
To-morrow'll be the happiest time of all the glad
    New-year;
Of all the glad New-year, mother, the maddest
    merriest day;
For I'm to be Queen o' the May, mother, I'm to be
    Queen o' the May.

I sleep so sound all night, mother, that I shall never
    wake
If you do not call me loud when the day begins to
    break:
But I must gather knots of flowers, and buds and
    garlands gay,
For I'm to be Queen o' the May, mother, I'm to be
    Queen o' the May.

Alfred Lord Tennyson

Tomorrow's the fair,
And I shall be there,
Stuffing my guts
With gingerbread nuts.

Traditional, English

THE CIRCUS

Friday came and the circus was there,
And Mother said that the twins and I
And Charles and Clarence and all of us
Could go out and see the parade go by.

And there were wagons with pictures on,
And you never could guess what they had inside,
Nobody could guess, for the doors were shut,
And there was a dog that a monkey could ride.

A man on the top of a sort of cart
Was clapping his hands and making a talk.
And the elephant came—he can step pretty far—
It made us laugh to see him walk.

Three beautiful ladies came riding by,
And each one had on a golden dress,
And each one had a golden whip,
They were queens of Sheba, I guess.

A big wild man was in a cage,
And he had some snakes going over his feet
And somebody said "He eats them alive!"
But I didn't see him eat.

Elizabeth Madox Roberts

Mother's Day

From: THE PEOPLE, YES

"I love you,"
said a great mother.
"I love you for what you are
knowing so well what you are.
And I love you more yet, child,
deeper yet than ever, child,
for what you are going to be,
knowing so well you are going far,
knowing your great works are ahead,
ahead and beyond,
yonder and far over yet."

Carl Sandburg

SAM'S WORLD

sam's mother has
grey combed hair

she will never touch
it with a hot iron

she leaves it
the way the lord
intended

she wears it proudly
a black and grey
round head of hair

Sam Cornish

THE GREAT MOTHER

Not all those who pass

In front of the Great Mother's chair

Get passt with only a stare.

Some she looks at their hands

To see what sort of savages they were.

Gary Snyder

MOTHER TO SON

Well, son, I'll tell you:
Life for me ain't been no crystal stair.
It's had tacks in it,
And splinters,
And boards torn up,
And places with no carpet on the floor—
Bare.
But all the time
I'se been a-climbin' on,
And reachin' landin's,
And turnin' corners,
And sometimes goin' in the dark
Where there ain't been no light.
So, boy, don't you turn back;
Don't you set down on the steps
'Cause you find it kinder hard.
Don't you fall now—
For I'se still goin', honey,
I'se still climbin',
And life for me ain't been no crystal stair.

Langston Hughes

When I am a man,
I shall be a hunter, O father,
I shall be a harpooner, O father,
I shall be a canoe-builder, O father,
I shall be an artisan, O father,
Then we shall not be in want, O father.
Ya, ha, ha, ha.

> *Kwakiutl* (American Indian, Vancouver)
> *Translated by Franz Boaz*

FATHER'S STORY

We put more coal on the big red fire,
And while we were waiting for dinner to cook,
Our father comes and tells us about
A story that he has read in a book.

And Charles and Will and Dick and I
And all of us but Clarence are there.
And some of us sit on Father's legs,
But one has to sit on the little red chair.

And when we are sitting very still,
He sings us a song or tells us a piece;
He sings Dan Tucker Went to Town,
Or he tells us about the golden fleece.

He tells about the golden wool,
And some of it is about a boy
Named Jason, and about a ship,
And some is about a town called Troy.

And while he is telling or singing it through,
I stand by his arm, for that is my place.
And I push my fingers into his skin
To make little dents in his big rough face.

Elizabeth Madox Roberts

FATHER

Carrying my world
Your head tops ceilings.
Your shoulders split door frames.
Your back holds up walls.

You are bigger than all sounds of laughter,
                                of weeping,
Your hand in mine keeps us straight ahead.

Myra Cohn Livingston

THAT DARK OTHER MOUNTAIN

My father could go down a mountain faster than I
Though I was first one up.
Legs braced or with quick steps he slid
    the gravel slopes
Where I picked cautious footholds.

Black, Iron, Eagle, Doublehead, Chocorus,
Wildcat and Carter Dome—
He beat me down them all. And that last
    other mountain,
And that other dark mountain.

Robert Francis

The Fourth of July

FOURTH OF JULY NIGHT

Pin wheels whirling round
Spit sparks upon the ground,
And rockets shoot up high
And blossom in the sky—
Blue and yellow, green and red
Flowers falling on my head,
And I don't ever have to go
To bed, to bed, to bed!

Dorothy Aldis

THE FOURTH

Oh
CRASH!
my
BASH!
it's
BANG!
the
ZANG!
Fourth
WHOOSH!
of
BAROOOM!
July
WHEW!

Shel Silverstein

74

From: SONG OF THE BANNER AT DAYBREAK

CHILD

Father what is that in the sky beckoning to me with long
        finger?
And what does it say to me all the while?
            . . .
O father it is alive—it is full of people—it has children,
O now it seems to me it is talking to its children,
I hear it—it talks to me—O it is wonderful!
O it stretches—it spreads and runs so fast—O my father,
It is so broad it covers the whole sky.
            . . .
                    . . . O father dear, that banner
    I like,
That pennant I would and must be.

Walt Whitman

JULY

Everett Anderson thinks he'll make
America a birthday cake
only the sugar is almost gone
and payday's not till later on.

Lucille Clifton

FOURTH OF JULY

Fat torpedoes in bursting jackets,
Firecrackers in scarlet packets.
We'll be up at crack o' day,
Fourth of July——Hurray! Hooray!

Rachel Field

FIREWORKS

First
a far thud,
Then the rocket
Climbs the air,
A dull red flare,
To hang, a moment,
Invisible, before
Its shut black shell cracks
And claps against the ears,
Breaks and billows into bloom,
Spilling down clear green sparks, gold spears,
Silent sliding silver waterfalls and stars.

Valerie Worth

From: GOOD NIGHT

Many ways to spell good night.

Fireworks at a pier on the Fourth of July
    spell it with red wheels and yellow spokes.
They fizz in the air, touch the water and quit.
Rockets make a trajectory of gold-and-blue
    and then go out.

Carl Sandburg

THE 5TH OF JULY

The moon moved over last night
      for bright sprays of fire
      big bursts of light.
      Fountains and candles
      and rockets zoomed by
      which seemed that they might
      burn some holes in the sky.

And the crowd cried "Aaah!"
      at the blinding displays
      of orbital pinwheels
      multiple rays
      that built to the final
      spectacular shower
      that made the plain night
      a sky-garden in flower.

Now, there's an arc of leftover light
      caught in the dark
      trapped by the night
      with pieces about it
      dotting the sky—
      a remembrance
      of the 4th of July.

Felice Holman

REFUGEE IN AMERICA

There are words like freedom,
Sweet and wonderful to say.
On my hearstrings freedom sings
All day everyday.

There are words like brotherhood
That almost make me cry.
If you had known what I've known
You'd know why.

Langston Hughes

Columbus Day

MYSTERIOUS BIOGRAPHY

Christofo Colombo was a hungry man,
hunted himself half way round the world;
he began poor, panhandled, ended in jail,
Christofo so hungry, Christofo so poor,
Christofo in the chilly, steel bracelets,
honorable distinguished Christofo Colombo.

Carl Sandburg

12 OCTOBER

From where I stand now
    the world is flat,
    flat out flat,
    no end to that.

    Where my eyes go the land moves out.

    How is it then
    five hundred years ago (about)
    Columbus found
    that far beyond the flat on flat
    the world was round?

Myra Cohn Livingston

From: RELIGION BACK HOME

4) When my little brother chanted,
    "In 1492 Jesus crossed the ocean blue,"
    Mother said, "Bob, you mean
    Columbus crossed the ocean blue."
    And he said, "I always did get
    them two guys mixed up."

                                    William Stafford

Halloween

From: SUPPOSE YOU MET A WITCH

Suppose you met a witch . . . . There's one I know,
all willow-gnarled and whiskered head to toe.
We drownded her at Ten Foot Bridge
last June, I think—
but I've seen her often since at twilight time
under the willows by the river brink,
skimming the wool-white meadow mist
astride her broom o'beech.
And once, as she flew past, with a sudden twist
and flick of the stick she whisked me in
head over heels, splash in the scummy water
up to my chin—
ugh! . . .
Yet there are witless folk will say
they don't exist.

Ian Serraillier

PUMPKIN

After its lid
Is cut, the slick
Seeds and stuck
Wet strings
Scooped out,
Walls scraped
Dry and white,
Face carved, candle
Fixed and lit,

Light creeps
Into the thick
Rind: giving
That dead orange
Vegetable skull
Warm skin, making
A live head
To hold its
Sharp gold grin.

Valerie Worth

hist   whist
little ghostthings
tip-toe
twinkle-toe

little twitchy
witches and tingling
goblins
hob-a-nob   hob-a-nob

little hoppy happy
toad in tweeds
tweeds
little itchy mousies

with scuttling
eyes   rustle and run   and
hidehidehide
whisk

whisk   look out for the old woman
with the wart on her nose
what she'll do to yer
nobody knows

for she knows the devil   ooch
the devil   ouch
the devil
ach   the great

green
dancing
devil
devil

devil
devil

    wheeEEE

e.e. cummings

WE THREE

We three
went out on Halloween,
A Pirate
An Ape
A Witch between.

We went from door to door.

By the light
of the moon
these shadows were seen
A Pirate
An Ape
A Witch between
and——

Say, how did we got to be FOUR?

Lilian Moore

HALLOWE'EN

Tonight is the night
When dead leaves fly
Like witches on switches
Across the sky,
When elf and sprite
Flit through the night
On a moony sheen.

Tonight is the night
When leaves make a sound
Like a gnome in his home
Under the ground,
When spooks and trolls
Creep out of holes
Mossy and green.

Tonight is the night
When pumpkins stare
Through sheaves and leaves
Everywhere,
When ghoul and ghost
And goblin host
Dance round their queen.
It's Hallowe'en!

Harry Behn

HALLOWEEN WITCHES

Magical prognosticator,
Chanting, canting, calculator,
Exorcist and necromancer,
Venificial, sabbat dancer,
Striga, arted and capricious,
Conjurer and *maleficius.*

Tonight, how many witches fly?
How many brooms will sweep the sky?

Felice Holman

From: A CORNISH LITANY

From Ghoulies and Ghosties,
And long-leggity Beasties,
And all Things that go bump in the Night,
Good Lord deliver us.

Traditional, English

Thanksgiving

AN INDIAN HYMN OF THANKS TO MOTHER CORN

I

See! The Mother Corn comes hither, making all
        hearts glad!
Making all hearts glad!
Giving her thanks, she brings a blessing; now,
        behold! she is here!

II

Yonder Mother Corn is coming, coming unto us!
Coming unto us!
Peace and plenty she is bringing; now, behold!
        she is here!

American Indian, Pawnee

From: I WILL GO WITH MY FATHER A-PLOUGHING

I will go with my father a-reaping
To the brown field by the sea,
And the geese and the crows and the children
Will come flocking after me.
I will sing to the tan-faced reapers,
With the wren in the heat of the sun,
And my father will sing the scythe-song
That joys for the harvest done.

Joseph Campbell

FIRST THANKSGIVING

Three days we had,
    feasting, praying, singing.

Three days outdoors at wooden tables,
Colonists and Indians together,
Celebrating a full harvest,
A golden summer of corn.

    We hunted the woods, finding
    Venison, deer, and wild turkey.

    We brought our plump geese and ducks,
    Great catches of silver fish.

    We baked corn meal bread with nuts,
    Journey cake, and steaming succotash.

    We roasted the meat on spits
    Before huge, leaping fires.

    We stewed our tawny pumpkins
    In buckets of bubbling maple sap.

Three days we had,
    feasting, praying, singing.

Three days outdoors at wooden tables,
Colonists and Indians together,
Celebrating a full harvest,
Praying, each to our God.

Myra Cohn Livingston

HARVEST SONG

O reapers and gleaners,
Come dance in the sun:
The last sheaves are stocked,
And the harvest is done.

The thistle-finch sings,
And the corn-plover cries,
And the bee and the moth
Flit about in the skies.

For Jesus has quickened
The seed in the mould,
And turned the green ears
Of the summer to gold.

The hill-folk all winter
Have clamoured for bread,
And here is enough
For a host to be fed!

Last year was a lean year,
And this is a fat,
And poor folk have cause
To be thankful for that.

So, reapers and gleaners,
Come dance in the sun,
And praise Mary's Child
That the harvest is done.

Joseph Campbell

Christmas

Christmas is coming. The geese are getting fat.
Please to put a penny in the old man's hat.
If you haven't got a penny, a ha'penny will do,
If you haven't got a ha'penny, God bless you.

Traditional, English

CAROL OF THE BROWN KING

Of the three Wise Men
Who came to the King,
One was a brown man,
So they sing.

Of the three Wise Men
Who followed the Star,
One was a brown king
From afar.

They brought fine gifts
Of spices and gold
In jeweled boxes
Of beauty untold.

Unto His humble
Manger they came
And bowed their heads
In Jesus' name.

Three wise Men,
One dark like me—
Part of His
Nativity.

Langston Hughes

CHRISTMAS MORNING

Christmas bells, awake and ring
Your carol of long ago,
Awake O wintry sun and fling
Your beams across the snow!

Children, merrily merrily sing
That all the world may know
Today the angels earthward swing
To bless us here below!

Harry Behn

What can I give Him,
   Poor as I am?
If I were a shepherd
   I would bring a lamb,
If I were a Wise Man
   I would do my part,—
Yet what can I give Him,
   Give my heart.

Christina Rossetti

FOR ALLAN

Who wanted to see how I wrote
a poem

Among these mountains, do you know,
I have a farm, and on it grow
A thousand lovely Christmas trees.
I'd like to send you one of these,
But it's against the laws.
A man may give a little boy
A book, a useful knife, a toy,
Or even a rhyme like this by me
 (I wrote it just like this you see) ,
But nobody may give a tree
Excepting Santa Claus.

Robert Frost

little tree
little silent Christmas tree
you are so little
you are more like a flower

who found you in the green forest
and were you very sorry to come away?
see   i will comfort you
because you smell so sweetly

i will kiss your cool bark
and hug you safe and tight
just as your mother would,
only don't be afraid

look   the spangles
that sleep all the year in a dark box
dreaming of being taken out and allowed to shine,
the balls the chains red and gold the fluffy threads,

put up your little arms
and i'll give them all to you to hold
every finger shall have its ring
and there won't be a single place dark or unhappy

then when you're quite dressed
you'll stand in the window for everyone to see
and how they'll stare!
oh but you'll be very proud

and my little sister and i will take hands
and looking up at our beautiful tree
we'll dance and sing
"Noel Noel"

e.e. cummings (American, 1894–1962)

CHRISTMAS EVE

My stocking's where
He'll see it—there!
One-half a pair.

The tree is sprayed,
My prayers are prayed,
My wants are weighed.

I've made a list
Of what he missed
Last year. I've kissed

My father, mother,
Sister, brother;
I've done those other

Things I should
And would and could.
So far, so good.

David McCord

From: FATHER FOX'S PENNYRHYMES

Apples for the little ones
And sweets for Christmas morn,
A dear blue bonnet for my wife
And I love barley corn.

Clyde Watson

CHRISTMAS MORNING

If Bethlehem were here today,
Or this were very long ago,
There wouldn't be a winter time
Nor any cold or snow.

I'd run out through the garden gate,
And down along the pasture walk;
And off beside the cattle barns
I'd hear a kind of gentle talk.

I'd move the heavy iron chain
And pull away the wooden pin;
I'd push the door a little bit
And tiptoe very softly in.

The pigeons and the yellow hens
And all the cows would stand away;
Their eyes would open wide to see
A lady in the manger hay,

If this were very long ago
And Bethlehem were here today.

And Mother held my hand and smiled—
I mean the lady would—and she
Would take the woolly blankets off
Her little boy so I could see.

His shut-up eyes would be asleep,
And he would look like our John,
And he would be all crumpled too,
And have a pinkish color on.

I'd watch his breath go in and out.
His little clothes would all be white.
I'd slip my finger in his hand
To feel how he could hold it tight.

And she would smile and say, "Take care,"
The mother, Mary, would, "Take care";
And I would kiss his little hand
And touch his hair.

While Mary put the blankets back
The gentle talk would soon begin.
And when I'd tiptoe softly out
I'd meet the wise men going in.

Elizabeth Madox Roberts

OTTO

It's Christmas Day. I did not get
The presents that I hoped for. Yet,
It is not nice to frown or fret.

To frown or fret would not be fair.
My Dad must never know I care
It's hard enough for him to bear.

Gwendolyn Brooks

I SAW THREE SHIPS

I saw three ships come sailing in,
  On Christmas Day, on Christmas Day,
I saw three ships come sailing in,
  On Christmas Day in the morning.

And what was in those ships all three?
  On Christmas Day, on Christmas Day,
And what was in those ships all three?
  On Christmas Day in the morning.

Our Saviour Christ and his lady.
  On Christmas Day, on Christmas Day,
Our Saviour Christ and his lady.
  On Christmas Day in the morning.

Pray, whither sailed those ships all three?
  On Christmas Day, on Christmas Day,
Pray, whither sailed those ships all three?
  On Christmas Day in the morning.

O, they sailed into Bethlehem.
  On Christmas Day, on Christmas Day,
O, they sailed into Bethlehem.
  On Christmas Day in the morning.

And all the bells on earth shall ring,
  On Christmas Day, on Christmas Day,
And all the bells on earth shall ring,
  On Christmas Day in the morning.

And all the angels in Heaven shall sing,
  On Christmas Day, on Christmas Day,
And all the angels in Heaven shall sing,
  On Christmas Day in the morning.

And all the souls on earth shall sing.
  On Christmas Day, on Christmas Day,
And all the souls on earth shall sing.
  On Christmas Day in the morning.

Then let us all rejoice amain!
  On Christmas Day, on Christmas Day,
Then let us all rejoice amain!
  On Christmas Day in the morning.

Old English Carol

Index

TRANSLATORS